MUSCLE MEMORIES OF LOVE AND DISASTER

TIM MAYO

Bainbridge Island Press

MUSCLE MEMORIES OF LOVE AND DISASTER

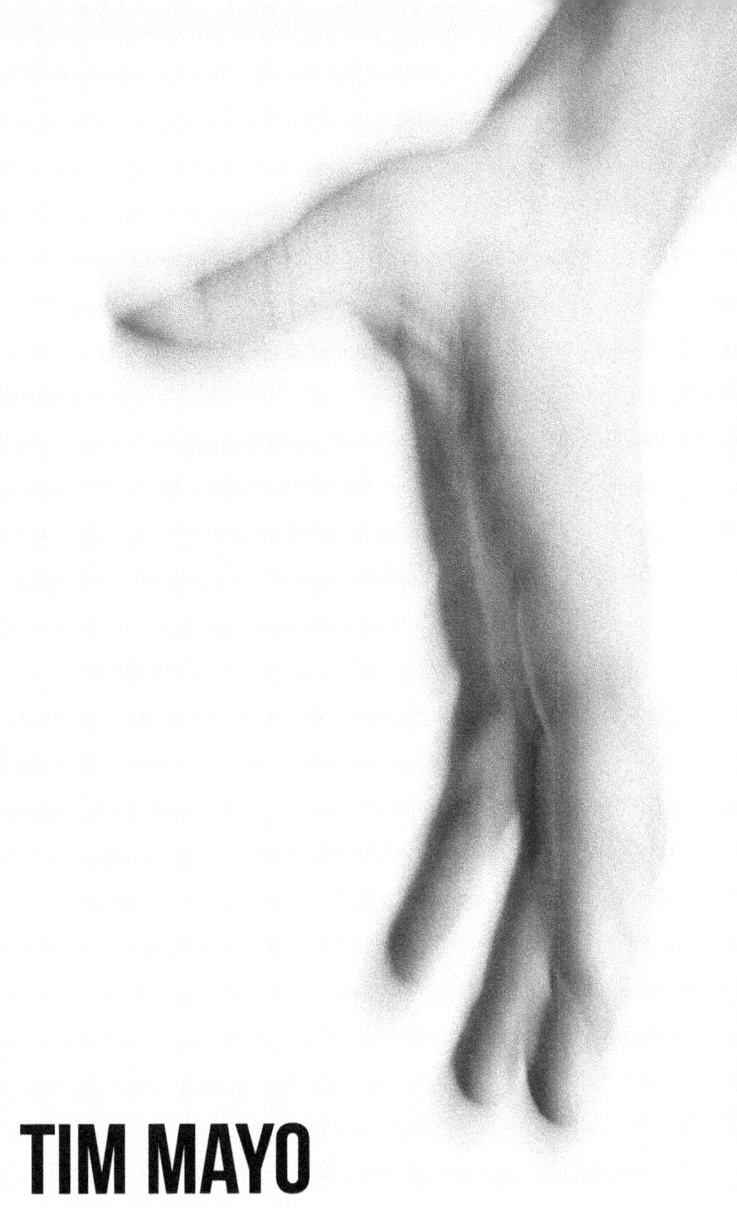

TIM MAYO

Bainbridge Island Press

Bainbridge Island, WA

Muscle Memories of Love and Disaster
by Tim Mayo
Copyright © 2026
All rights reserved

Published in 2026 by Bainbridge Island Press
Bainbridge Island, WA
https://bainbridgeisland.press

Printed in the United States of America

ISBN: 978-1-961451-15-5
Library of Congress Control Number: 2026931444

Cover & Book Design: Ben Rockwood

9 8 7 6 5 4 3 2 1

Yet I think of you, now, only you,
and not myself, my own less pain-racked body
aching in the dark with its muscle memories
of love and disaster.

For Patricia Fargnoli
(Nov. 16, 1937 – Feb. 18, 2021)

For My Daughter
(Jan. 23, 1965 – Jun. 30, 2023)

Again, for Amelia Hancock
(Nov. 1, 1961 – Mar. 13, 2013)

And definitely for Betsy, my muse

Contents

MUSCLE MEMORIES OF LOVE AND DISASTER

Landscape with Still Life

The blue heron tilting its way
away from us into the tawny,

clustered stilts of reeds,
finally, the reeds, themselves,

their purple flowers blonding
in the autumn sun.

All this reflection
in a looking-glass calm.

We die . . . we die . . .
nothing new there.

But what we want
is to re-envision the wilting

flowers perking back
to full bloom, luminous

and still in their vase,
the rabbit and the pheasant

unhooking themselves
from the hunter's door,

each shuddering its way back
to the quick in a hop and a flap.

What we get, instead,
is the circumspect blue heron

reappearing in leggy defiance,
the reeds now fully arranged

behind it like a chorus,
as it fearlessly steps toward us,

the slow, erratic dip
and ess of its neck posing

the same question again and again.

The Gospel of Numbers Not in Service

I always answer the first time they call,
and in that long hush before I hang up,
I conjure up their diaphanous faces all
milky with the sadness of the disembodied,
and I see their translucent lips open and
close, their jaws stiff as hooked fish
in the suffocating air where they float.

I imagine them desperately mouthing
for their forgotten voices to return, then
miming with an unmentionable veracity
their plight of not being serviced, or even
carping about their banishment to this blur
of space somewhere between oblivion
and the hum-less ha-ha of prankster calls.

In the end, I don't know what they want.
Maybe they just want to commiserate
about the slow disconnect of my late
love, whose small, piping voice I've kept
all these years in a digital urn, waiting
for her substance to return, to show
and tell the good news only the dead know.

June Burial

To Patricia Fargnoli

At last, June cedes its drooping peonies to the black
armies of ants, and I am trying to think what flowers
come next in this sad season. I've always loved lilacs,
but we're way past their time, and way, way past forsythia
spackling the rising whips of their stalks with yellow petals
before disappearing into a green tardiness of leaves.
Why am I going backwards, like those flowers,
which blossom before leafing, and choosing with each
bloom an earlier time? Soon I will arrive back at the point
of your leaving, where no flowers bloomed, both of us staring
at the bare back of March as we try to pass it by, me thinking
of summer, you the impending black ants searching for
the cancerous sweet nectar of sleep, while we still
stamp our feet in the snow.

And so, I conjure up bumble

bees curling their awkward, furry bodies into the rumpled
sheets of dying peonies, and we are back in June, and I am
at your grave with a woman I love by my side. I am so glad
for her friendship since I've lost yours, so glad for that long
stretch of time I've known her, dating back beyond so many
seasons of peonies, forsythia, back as far as my adolescence.
(My god. A woman I've known that long.) I can almost say
I grew up with her, even though I've never grown up.
She's not a lover, nor a wife. She is here for you, dear friend.
And perhaps for me, too. I would offer you her sorrow, her
solace, along with my grief, if I could. I would offer them
in a bouquet alongside the transience of these day lilies with
their long necks leaning over the road we've traveled as if
curious to see which way we came, which way we've gone.

Meditation on Your Final Moment

For Pat Fargnoli

For me, maybe that moment is a heightened state
slackened to a palatable point, where body
and brain can balance before the end. Or is it
possibly . . . just a state of immense relief?
No, it must be more, although I'd settle for that.
Any old port in the storm as they say. But for you,
the poet in me wants something more out-of-body,
where, when it fans its feathers before your eyes,
your jaw just drops and you're there.

In some stories that must be how it happens:
an affirmation of the holy spirit extends its wing
like the hand of God. But in the flesh and blood world?
A bird before your eyes, and *bingo!* you've suddenly
bounced off the bottom of your life ascending
into the air of who-knows-where? Not a chance.

So let us then think of the practical how,
the mechanics to move you to your end without needing
some bureaucratic benediction, some absolution,
or a passport for your pale ghosts of regret.
Maybe all you need is just a gentle,
saline solution of generosity
flushing the blood right out of your veins—
I mean, why not? It feels right
in its medically nonjudgmental *soulagement,**
the cool liquid diffusing the fever that was
the passionate red of your life's discomfort.
Your *salut** in all its meanings as you greet
the penultimate experience of your life.

The soul—I hate to say the word—twisted with the wishes
and wants of this world—I hate to say it, because
nothing's immortal except the stone base of the universe—
the soul, as your seeing-eye dog sensing everything you can't,
wants its way to where the flesh isn't in the way.

Christ! How did I get here? Talking like this.
I'm not a believer. Yet I think of you, now, only you,
and not myself, my own less pain-racked body
aching in the dark with its muscle memories
of love and disaster. I think of you reaching
for this timeless moment, and I ask why not
pass these last moments of your life in that grace
of letting go, that anti-struggle to faith? But I know
you're waiting for some ecstatic flash of mind to happen
before the big sigh you only have to exhale once
lifts you to the wherever you've always wanted to be.

Who cares whether it's real or not?
Won't that breath be worth it?

* *soulagement* is French for relief, and *salut* has two meanings in French, the first
is as a greeting and the second meaning is salvation.

The People Inside Me:

my Mediterranean, foster sister (still alive)
her face hardened like sun-dried tomatoes
before my eyes as her mother softened
into French toast and tears when I left;

my adoptive mother, whose husband slipped
behind the Iron Curtain as she knelt by my bed
as if in prayer for her nightly confession, drunk
on the connectivity of her disconnection;

my own mother, years later, asking me about
military school, as she uncrossed her leg, and I,
ever the red-blooded cadet, maneuvered to peek
up her skirt, not knowing she was my mother;

my father, whom I don't remember, whose face
I now wear like a hand-me-down, the bright
troth on his wedding finger for someone else
winking back in the one photo we're both in;

my stepfather, whose boyishness belied adulthood
as we snuck down to the basement to shoot his guns,
and that one bullet which missed the phone book
and ricocheted back between us as we laughed;

and finally, my old friend, John, who each year
walked slower and slower always looking
about himself as if to make note of the air
one last time before he turned to dust.

To My Foster Sister, Late in Life

For Simone

In the dreamlessness of my todays,
thoughtless times when the air fills
with a puff of loss the breeze brings in

cooling the lonely heat of the moment,
when its emptiness surrounds me,

then scurries on into the bustling tempo:
the daily task of tasking myself daily
to keep the demons from my door,
the chug and clamor of work, eat, worry,
sleep, *think* love—not love, get the car fixed,
then back to the same work, eat, worry, fix car
to move away from the et cetera of my days,

I repeat, under my breath, *you* are the earthy
root I stub my toe on whenever I look away.

You are the ghost of might have been
who has followed me from a distance
called the other life I never had . . .

The Anthropology of Old Age

Recently, I've passed into a neighborhood,
where everyone knows their neighbor.
Wrinkles populate their faces like tribal scars,
although, for the most part, their eyes are bright
as ever. They're friendly and very talkative.

Still learning their language, I say little: I smile,
make an occasional, commiserative grimace, mime
all the expected gestures that come with words.

They, in turn, seem patient, attentive to my clucks
and shrugs, as if they know, in the end, validation
courses through my veins, accepting them as they
are, despite my hesitance to voice my thoughts.

Evening comes, the daily chatter ends,
and everyone retreats inside,
counting in silence the days that are left.

I am still learning their mating habits,
though progeny is no longer their purpose,
learning the attitudes towards their now-grown
young, and those little people with large eyes,
who curl into their laps like folded hands.

Variations on Mozart's Rondo in A Minor

(As played by Murray Perahia)

In Mozart's rondo, you hear the opening strains
trip like a child just learning to walk:
unsteady but tickled by each onward step.

Even the untrained listener can hear this
and imagine the look-at-me-smile of uncertain
mastery as the fingers of the pianist hesitate

then continue nimbly over the keys.
The melody goes on, descends into sadness
like a parent who knows exactly when the child

will fall and why. But just as you consider this
modulating *tristesse*, the music turns abruptly
to another place beyond the child's first steps,

beyond even the parent's sadness,
and you behold in your mind's eye—in your hands—
a delicate globe of a miniature domain,

where the bent woodcutter from some forgotten tale
trudges knee-deep through a snow-filled meadow,
wading to his hut from the sprigs of green forest;

the day's deeds committed and done,
everything still swirls about, then settles into this
final clarity, which clouds only if you budge.

At the Chemo Clinic

It's been several years since I went, and I went only once
to accompany my daughter. So, now, as I try to dredge up
the details to tell you or to tell anyone who, unafflicted,
does not suffer, though we all do in our different ways,
my memory melds the moment with my imagination,
makes of it something other than it is or was.

Picture yourself out for your ritual Sunday drive,
and you need gas, so, you pull in to your local Exxon
to fill up your body for a trip to an aimless place,
circling around the lake of regret, asking yourself
why you didn't do this before, cruising on through
the neighborhood of wistfulness. What can I say?

I remember the twitter of small talk in the treatment room.
How it echoed like spring, surprising me with its sound,
as, armed with her pillow, book, and cellphone, my daughter
picked a private spot to wait for the attendant nurse to come,
attach the clear plastic hose to her chest and start the pump,
so I could see how prayer poured into the hourglass of her heart.

Vicissitudes

Yainfrumarounhéa, said the hitchhiker. I thought
about his ear for accent, as I planned my answer:
how I'd lived here twice as long as he'd been alive,
that I knew more than he did about the land he'd been
born to, but I kept my counsel. He was poorer than I,
unread, though the leaves of trees were a library to him.
No car, or at least none that worked, and a home too
complicated to hitch to: down this dirt road to that one
after all the asphalt he would have had to travel
from where he worked to get there, but he was going
the other way. So, once out of the woods, he thumbed.
I'd done that, too, walked miles to the macadam
then hoped my way.
                  Still, I wasn't the same as him.
I no longer hoped, and my speech was too crisp
and learned, my words distinctly differentiated,
not slurred together into one, long word-of-a-sentence
with consonants lopped off and vowels lilting against
what's left to make my speech harmonious to his ear.
Yet I understood his remark wasn't meant as accusation.
Thankful for the ride, he wanted to make his small
talk with a stranger into something bigger, something
that could connect us over the long bridge we were
crossing in my car, him on his way to work,
me on my way home, as I now lived in town
on a paved street instead of a hardpan road.

The Black Wolf of Your Past

Suppose you do change your life,
and the black wolf,

which was once your shadow,
silently howls against this extinction.

What do you *then* do for this feral
darkness out of which you grew,

which has trailed you all your life
with a loyalty reserved for pets?

You see it cower, shrink back—deep
into the dog-house of your thoughts,

the long leash of its reach diminished.

What do you do for this wolf
you have fed since birth . . .

throw it a bone?

Another Man's Treasure

Out of the boredom of rainy-day Sundays,
yet again, I descend the dank cellar stairs.
Today, beneath a tepee of skis, I discover
a velvet sack in a plastic shopping bag
brittle with age. At first, I don't recall it.
Then I recognize inside the sack
the wooden, cube-shaped urn,
which carried to this shore the ashes of my friend,
who now rests among the roots of a pear tree
beside his brother's house.
We didn't talk for years,
our friendship shattered into shards,
then reglued itself as if nothing had happened.

When his widow brought him home, she
couldn't bear to rid herself of the urn's burden,
instead entrusting its emptiness to me. I hesitated
thinking of the sacrilege of my options:
driving it to the dump, or just lobbing it
into any dumpster I might pass by.
Now, peeling back the sack's velvet lip,
I see the chipped remains of red wax
used to seal the lid. Lifting it, I see another,
white, plastic bag inside, more durable
than the first, its interior powdered with ash.
Rummaging beneath it, I find the brass screws
which had kept the box and my friend intact,
and finally, this one, last object:

       an off-white,

plaster of Paris medallion,
a number stamped on its face
and a date on the back.
The year my friend died.
I heft it once again in my hand,
and in the cellar's quiet dimness,

this portal to both our lives,
I imagine an artifact whose purpose must
have been a passport to the afterlife,
a brittle document issued by some ancient
Sumerian bureaucrat or priest and valid
only upon the bearer's expiration.
And I picture myself as this archaeologist,
who has searched his whole life for
some unaltered remnant of the past,
a hard constancy he could hold onto.

The Ladder

Thou shalt love thy neighbor as thyself
—Matthew 22:39

And you see yourself struggling up this ladder
toward some intangible paradigm of self-love,
painfully stepping up from each lower rung
of self-loathing to the next one
of lesser loathing, where you hope
to glimpse a kinder, gentler self,
save your soles this soreness of effort,
finally see the beauty in your angular,
asymmetrical face, your awkward gait,
and your slow ability to forgive yourself,

but the balls of your bare feet have become
so bruised by each rung's resistance
to your weight and purpose, you can hardly
step up anymore, just as the revelation
comes to you in that sudden balancing act
atop the ladder, now splayed, A-like,
to each side of you, where all the limits
of the room, walls, ceiling, floor, remain
out of reach, but somehow, the infinity
of love now seems within reach
in that yonder of an ideal world,

as there, in the wobbly stillness, you realize
how walking on air could be
the ultimate state, where the pain
of each step would no longer exist,
and the air would embrace you, every part of you,
right down to your black and blue soles,

and the air would embrace everyone—
even your neighbor, the one we haven't yet
addressed in this poem, who stands,
grounded, holding your ladder, tensing
every muscle to jump and catch you.

Hallway

You came home from work. In the hall, dim
with a flawless optimism such light lends,
you turned and looked in the mirror
with its umbrella stand below.

What was different about you?
How had you changed? Your patients
told you they loved you. Your presence
was calming. You were their antidote.

Before, you were neither loved nor hated.
You were just the person you were: incurable
in the evening, the fool at the bar,
the next morning, the young man

cashing his check at the bank
making small talk with the cashier
while lustful thoughts lurked behind
his blood-shot eyes. In those days

you didn't work at the hospital, you just lived.
Each day must have been the same, although
each must have differed from the day before
by being, in fact, the day after.

You looked at your face, your eyes looked back
unchanged but with a certain kindness
that a configuration of muscles had
molded into the lines of your face.

Your hair was graying at the temples.
You had spent your whole life turning
away from remembrance—away from all
the mirrors offering their umbrellas

to guard against the inclemency
of the outside world. Your life seemed
until that moment an unfilled blank
waiting to be remembered.

The Steel Gray Nail

I'm looking at a gray photograph
my foster sister sent me years ago,
set in a small, silver frame, dulled
by time and memory. In it, my foster
parents pose, clothed in their different
shades of gray clothes: *Albert* in his bib
overalls, that were really faded blue
from pushing wheelbarrows in the sun.
A loosely defined laborer by trade, he raked
clams in the waist-deep waters of the bay,
and pushed the weight of work—dirt,
cement—whatever needed to be moved
to the here and there of its final place,
then lullabied me to sleep at night.

Nannette standing beside him in her
seemingly charcoal and floral smock,
which was actually indigo with yellow
flowers splattered like suns against her
night-colored dress. Purse against her chest,
comptroller of the one-income family I left
not by choice but left nonetheless, what other
worries and sad losses did she carry in her
third bosom besides bills and bank books?

But the photo is as silent as it is gray
as they stand gray-haired against the asbestos
shingles of their house (which were, in fact,
gray). And today, I contemplate not the efficacy
of their home's armor against the weather,
but the world's unpredictable proclivities,
that shingles could not protect against,
the invisible people who controlled our lives,
when, at five, I jumped on a pile of broken
siding with all the rage of wanting to break
things because I had to leave, and the shingler,
who pulled the steel gray nail from my foot,
then carefully placed it in the small box
of my heart as if to say, *Remember this.*

The Moral of the Story

So, you've been working detox
for eight years seeing the repeat
business as a curse, grumbling
about how the clients never learn,
not knowing whatever happened
to all those you never see again.
What's wrong with this picture?
The pay's not bad—you're not
the head honcho—but you help people,
and the bennies are better than okay.

Anyway. You run into this guy
on the street. He kind of hops
around with one leg shorter
than the other, and he says
he knows you from work,
but you don't remember him,
and it's pretty clear why
as you listen to the way his whiney voice
seems to be asking for the love
no one ever gave him.

He's smaller than you are
and you're no giant.
But you listen, because that's
what you've learned to do,
and as you look down at him,
he thanks you with downcast eyes
for the many times you did listen
and for the wisdom of those poems
you used to read out loud
before each group you ran.

He tells you he's been sober, now,
for a year—just arrived back in town

and already he's got a night job
at the Sunoco near the interstate.
He jabbers on about how he spent the year
working at the Salvation Army, how he
begins and ends each day with a prayer
and all the minutia in between,
which have helped his spiritual growth.
He goes on and on until his speech
begins to feel a little forced, a little faster,
and you're not quite following him,
so you fix your eyes on the ground
as if this can help you listen.

Then, . . . he stops. . . . . .

You look up into his eyes; he winces
as he asks if you could help him
get a job like you have.
He wants to *give back a little,*
carry the message, as they say.

You can only imagine what your
wooden, professional face
must look like as you let this sink in,
and you think about how many years
you were sober before you began
this work, but he turns and hops away
before you can answer,

and as you watch him go, suddenly,
you think of Jiminy Cricket.

And then, you think of Pinocchio . . .
how he changed into a real boy at the end.

Big Nose Blond

For Betsy

Last night, McNeill's burned to the ground,
the brewery/bar at the bottom of the hill.
I remember a beer McNeill used to make
called Big Nose Blond. I think of salt,
when I try to taste it in my mind. Not
because it tasted salty, but my palate
recalls how it was the perfect antidote
for that bitter saltiness whenever some
aftertaste of life curdled on my tongue.
It would always be a recollection I couldn't
bear to enunciate almost like biting into
the liquidness of its memory, trying to
surround it with the hard consonants
of courage. And I remember a word
I never used, hidden in a ribbed cage,
which kept my heart from beating too fast,
from tearing itself apart for a reason I couldn't
fathom. A dangerous word, dangerous in
its velvet softness, a word I no longer fear
as I think of you in the dark of this morning,
before the dawn arrives, and I drive to work
with the memory of your hand in mine
as we walked toward the fire, where the big
nosed bottles rattled and popped in the flames.

A Pure Bodiless Sound

I'm thinking of the skylight in the cathedral
ceiling of your bedroom, how you told me
last night as we lay there about the moon
shining in the night before, and you couldn't sleep.
I remember saying, *you should've called me*,
but I was at work, where it was almost dead
until I gathered up my coat before shutting down
my lightless console, and a young woman called.
A crisis counselor. She didn't really want to know
if we had a bed for her suicidal client,
though that's what she asked. She just
wanted to hear a voice without a face, a pure
bodiless sound to soothe the strung-out chords
of her out-of-tune harp after arguing for hours
to keep a boy alive, who wanted with all
the anger of adolescence to die. I listened
and said a few words to help her get in tune again,
to straighten the tired feathers of her wings.
I even stayed on the line like a confessor,
an emissary from whatever light shines
in the dark closet of the confessional.
I listened right up to and past the hour
when work and I would both shut down,
calling it a night, and she, too, would
leave the emergency room for home
and the reel-to-reel replays she'd dream.

The business of poetry is not po-biz.

I want to say that to remind me how
profane the world can be, that even
the world of poetry can have this
life-goes-on side to it, Auden's dogs
going on with their doggy life, a humanity
of *who-cares?* seeping in between the lines.
And lastly, I want to add just one more thing.
I'm not a soft touch poet with a heart of gold,
who works in a mental hospital for love.
In my work boys always fall from the sky.
The trick is to let them land gently on the page,
where the moon I didn't see the other night
hangs by its slim thread, but still bright enough
to let me see you tossing in its light, restless
for all we wish for—even that boy's life.

The First Hurricane I Remember

I never saw. It came at night. We climbed
the attic stairs, to share twin beds tucked
under the roof's two hips. My foster sister
and I lay in separate beds each blanketed
in a parent. Then at dawn, kerosene lamp
in hand, our foster father ventured down.

I could only imagine the bay water slinking
along the kitchen floor like a wet shadow,
imagine it rising up to lick the dripping tap
above the sink where stacked dishes floated.

Still, I don't remember the brackish mud
smearing the greenness from the lawn
nor the keen bouquet of storm-fed jetsam
the jumbled world must have offered us.

Crumple Zone

*a part of a motor vehicle [. . .] designed to crumple easily in a crash
and absorb the main force of an impact.*
                              —New Oxford American Dictionary

Although I dream of freedom, flooring it
in reckless abandon like a breakneck bandit
ripping the day off from a standstill
in a squeal of smoking tires, reticence
impedes the gunning of my engine.
I could have been a renegade, a bear
dipping over my neighbor's empty dumpster,
a diurnal force of nature digging through
the ripe artifacts of a castaway human world,
huffing grumpy from no food
though the sniffing is always good.
But let's get back to me as a vehicle,
long off the assembly line,
rusting a bit at the rims,
yet still bragging about my design: how
all humans in the passenger place of my heart
travel well protected—even when
the turbulent world has bashed them
like a metal bear, the size of a semi
full of the prize of heavy hardware—
no light aluminum pots or pans there—
no-sirree-bob—all hammers and anvils—
freightage from the weighty manufactories
of a pre-plastic world—industry with a capital *I*—
large steel presses designed to stamp and
sizzle out mojo-horseshoes—fenders—bumpers—
and other hard luck charms for distribution.
That's what hit me, the makings of a better world.

Swan Song

It was finally evening in the new city, where I had chosen to live out my life. I was no longer in the country of my birth, but in a place, where language was new. I was like a babe listening to my own voice as it ran up and down the scales of all possible human sound. Or had I finally become the artist I'd hoped to be, rehearsing the consummate aria I had wanted all my life to sing? The sheer color of its melody and the ingenuity of its variations had thrilled me years ago when I'd first heard the famous prima donna on a worn out seventy-eight. At last, I would be able to give the world my own interpretation, though many thought I would not be able to reach those high ornamental notes the prima donna had so easily fluttered up to as if her voice were a butterfly alighting upon a new flower.

My studio overlooked a gated park, which still glistened from the early evening rain, and though I was cautioned to never go out in such air, I felt a need to clear my head of all my apprehensions. No sooner had I the passed through the gates, than I heard the distant sound of a barrel organ; I thought it odd to hear one playing so late, odder still that the melody was an off-kilter rendition of the aria I would soon perform. The cranking of the organ grinder lent an almost mocking rhythm to the music, always stopping at an unexpected place in the melody, then speeding up in what seemed an out-of-breath jumble of notes.

I followed the music until I came upon a small woman in a black shawl—one might even call her a crone—but that would be cruel. Her loose dress made it seem as if she had no body, and with each turn of the organ handle she hunched like a frightened cat then pressed her whole being downward employing what little heft she had to move the melody along. "Good evening, Madame." I nodded in return. The mist condensed on the pipes like tears, as she went on, "They say this melody is cursed, and those who perform it risk death. But surely that's an old wives' tale. After all, I've been playing this song for as long as I can remember, and memory is life."

The Sunshine

It's not like I had one of those episodes, where I
float through a tunnel to a bright and infinite room,
and I suddenly feel warm and fuzzy, as though
everything will be all right, because, now, I know
for sure there is a god (of sorts), an afterlife, _and_
I get to keep my cake and eat it, too. Then
the bright room fades away, because, being infinite,
it never had the necessary walls to keep me. Down
through the tunnel I retreat back into my small
wounded body to wake in a hospital, where a ceiling,
four walls, and a floor confine me.

                                All around me
loved ones are weeping; they mourn my imminent
departure from the touchable world, which had never
really touched me, though I can truly feel it now as hard
as the lump in my bed, poking me in the back, keeping
me from a good night's sleep. This is where I tell them
I've seen the light, that bright infinite room, and maybe
I add some more to the story like my dead mother, who
welcomes me with ragged arms, as she says, _it's alright._
So that's what I say, _it's alright, it's alright, end of story!_
And everyone stops crying, because I've had the vision,
and now I can depart in peace.

                              But in fact, I don't depart.
I stay here in this bed. I go on living, and I'm depressed
as hell, because my body is all bent and twisted, and I feel
this *can't-put-my-finger-on-it* discomfort pervading the air
like a fog with four broken limbs, floating in this unlit room
as I watch these damned, off-white ceiling tiles,
their peek-a-boo holes like beady entries to a dark world,
tiles I can't stop looking at, because I'm in this neck brace
with a tube down my throat *choking* me into breathing,
blocking my voice from bitching, and with another tube
poking out of my stomach to feed me drugs—all of this

meant to keep me painless, motionless, and complacent,
until I can feel—*who-the-hell-knows-when*—better
about the sunshine of shit luck and being alive.

A Different Color of Sun

When the nurse unbandaged my head, I
realized I couldn't speak in the old language;
the muscle of my mind knew no way to hold
the cleverness of its *bons mots*. All through
my body the ache of accident persisted.

          Reader,
you cannot know how I want this poem to end
in morning glories on the vine. But the best efforts
of my brain lead only to a spastic salute to life
made with my half-crippled arm raising its hand
to the swollen brow of my half-closed eye.
How can I tell you I've discovered in this new
language the infinite possibilities of pain & suffering
that exist in the universe? Yet my one open eye still
sees each pinprick blink of brightness called star
as the dark universe continues to expand.

          Friend,
I've come to the conclusion that suffering is the invisible
air we can't stop breathing; it surrounds the spirit
like the unconscious laying siege to our joy.
How can I tell you I awake each morning
to a different color of sun clawing at my window
like a dark tiger stalking my injured brain?

Self-Portrait with *Trache*

Grief is a black parrot in my throat.
He doesn't sing—he croaks,
my wired jaw his cage, then
through the small hole in my neck
he hawks a gob across the room.

What a pity! What a pity!
Put the pennies on the eyes.
Pieces of hate. Pieces of hate.
Close the box. Close the box.

His claws shuffle sideways.
Nothing can stop
his ruffled dance, his grip
on his precarious perch,
a wooden dowel as frail
as any bone in my body.

A Dark Visitor

> *This is the light of autumn; it has turned on us.*
> *Surely it is a privilege to approach the end*
> *still believing in something. —Louise Glück*

I am ending; like a lush green season
I fall into a brittle brown, a drowsiness.
Hip, neck, head, they're all broken.

Scared of the dark, even the afternoon light
slinks yellow through the window. A pastor
also came to visit; he was tall, commanding

a special presence by the way he stood:
head and shoulders above everyone.
I envied his towering demeanor

as if it signified a wisdom above mine.
Besides, a man of the cloth always carries
this mien in the mere weave of what

he wears. Yet I am still broken—no! I'm
more on the mend like a sock I need to darn.
They say tragedy happens next door,

and faith enters on faulty legs
like a newborn colt. Does it
ever learn to walk?

The Why Answers

Because I am an animal of the Universe
and the poem snakes through me
like a greased rope to woo you
in the garden of your soul

Because my spirit even surprises me,
the peek-a-boo, hide-and-seek of it,
when I arise to do poetry

Because the nurse is taking too long
and I will lose the best of these lines
to the medicine mixing meant to keep me alive

(Damn her slowness, her humble compassion,
her pure beauty for the love and art of caring)

Because the leg I shake dances across the Universe
in search of belief's star-burst, the momentary nova
blasting to eureka without end

Because the goddess of my life is a muse
who beckons when I least want her
yet I follow her now more than ever

Because the black hole that sucks me into
the misery of my past, where I love to wallow,
has suddenly lost its gravity, and I laugh with joy

Because the poem has become my prayer
and poetry my only cult, and I pray
to lose the curse that follows me
like a dog-loyal, best friend

Because suddenly I want to love in a way
I never knew, no ifs and buts about it,
compassion is the tail that wags my dog

Because it has taken this long to taste
the sweet nectar the allergy bearing bees,
who could kill me, carry like seraphim
and I want more—ah yes—I want more

Because there is no prey that doesn't
whimper *love me, love me, love me*
and no predator that doesn't love back
and I am the hunter and the hunted

Because I have learned a little thing
I can never forget: that the child
knows the inarticulate human need
all poets try to speak

Pine Heights Rehab

Although broken bones anchor me
to this moment, looking out the window
at the pines which name this place, I lay
on this bed half-crippled by memory.

Years ago, my lover died here; the room
was just like this, the floor's off-white tiles
designed to be wiped clean of those messy
colors the dying often leave behind.

And I remember how those same trees
shed their sharp green needles as she passed
falling as I did into that pathetic fallacy.
What have I learned since then?

That grief heats its molten heart
in a muscled cauldron, then hardens,
becomes as brittle as old bones
but never leaves the body.

A Candle For

After the half-life
of my daughter's last year
a dimness appeared

like a veiled busker
sawing out sad tunes
on her violin

The few pieces of silver
glinting up from the dark
velvet of her case

made me think of moons

Remembrance mirrors
the invisible of someone
so a self seems immortal

a thing which zigs beyond
its now-pulseless zag
to exit flesh and hover

at least a part of forever
but a candle can
only glimmer until

snuff it just sputters out

Porcupine Stew

For Sydney Lea

This is my bonfire lit for you on this longest night of the year.
It burns in the dark like those poems of yours, where winter's
a dying stove, a page of cold you're snowshoeing across,
where it's always so far below zero, but you still want to stay
in the cold *Here* of now to evade the colder moment to come.
Your poems remind me of when I, too, lived out of town
in an old farmhouse. They're all drafty, those houses,
drafty as I am full of the long wind of my stories—
but I'm getting away from the gist of this poem,
which concerns the porcupine I shot out of a pine tree
one winter solstice afternoon thinking it was a bear,
then left behind, because, after all, it was a porcupine.

That night, my folksy hunter-housemate, a cook by trade,
told me I should have brought it home and went on and on
about the porcupine stew we'd make. . . . So, fortified with rum,
I snowshoed out those two moonlit miles: past the fox's den,
smelling of skunk, on past the hemlocks creaking in the cold,
and the wild apples with one or two fruit still hanging brown
on the bough until I saw its body at the bottom of the tree:
all stiff in the white gleam and curled black into that frozen ball
of bristle and quills it had become. Still, I grabbed its tail
in my gloved hand just as the moon slid behind some clouds,
and I trudged back down the darkened woods road, snow
now my only light, the sound of my rackets whispering
a little heavier in the cold powder. All the way back
to more rum and the drafty warmth of an old farmhouse.

I think of you, Syd, as I dress this story on a slab,
as I finally confess we never made the stew
and my regret for killing this fellow creature.
And then I think of the stew of old age you and I
have both sunk into, all ghost-white like lumps
of potatoes, a stew that no porcupine can prick us
out of—that sad beast with its thousand quills
I should've at least tried to use for poems dipping
them into the inkwells puddling beneath the pines,
where the moon like a bright and final angel
can't reach either of us on this longest night.

Snow

Today it's snowing. You hate it
for reminding you of the page,
that ultimate white-out.
Later, much later, the sun

will come out, the snow will blind you,
and your head will ache as the white hurt
your eyes feel leaves you groping
in the dazzle of its sheer brilliance.

When you were young,
impervious to the cold, the night
below zero, you'd go to the dim
woodshed, barehanded,

to split wood. Now, you wonder
why you did it, why you let the frost
enter your hands, though the baby fat
of your zeal stopped its spread.

Funny how you can forget the odd
things you did when you were young
with nothing really to do.
Can't sleep? Split wood. Why not?

You used to like the snow, the soft, cold
hammer of it, the challenge it seemed to pose
like the deer in the backyard waiting to see
what kind of animal you really are.

A Father's Lament

We almost never met
but at eleven you asked

I forced a truce of sorts
conceded your fidelity

The years huddled like orphans
between the now-and-thens

And the clock's hand
scythed down

the might-have-beens
leaving only the likely

In the end I learned too late
the unconditional of surrender

Love in the Time of Accidents

When my daughter saw me, neck
brace keeping my lower lip stiff
instead of the proverbial upper,

I saw for the first time a fear of loss
crumple the freckles on her face
and open wide her hazel-green eyes.

It's not that I don't know loss, it was
my middle name for most my life
until I finally managed to lose it,

sloughing it off like the loosened skin
a snake sheds, then slithers on, oblivious
of what it's left behind. But how could I

speak to her of that ease? How loss lifts
burdens one never knew they carried.

Little Elegy, Inside Out
For My Daughter

You are now the blossoming tree
outside, still stalwart, whose
shadow enters our house.

Tell it slant, Emily always said.
Poems are only shadows—in fact,
all our words are just that.

We turn from the window
to our room inside;
behind us, the wind gusts.

One-two-three, one-two-
three, and there you are:
dancing in our house.

Amelia's Cat

On those final days when my lover
lay unhooked in her hospital bed,
hovering between the heavenly bodies
of life and death, I would travel

the Earth to her place, where the cat,
curled in a window, slept and waited
for sustenance with yawning
ambivalence and a hunter's hunger.

Sated, she would then stretch out
to the ends of her claws as if grasping
at the small feathers of air
trying to enter the closed window.

And I'd begin to hum a lullaby
to keep her company, some tune
I'd only just remembered from that
speechless part of life called infancy.

Day in and day out I would do this,
then open the window to fill the room
with earthly noises while the cat toyed
with the fluttering air like a wounded bird.

Brainectomy

1.

Brainectomy: a word coined by those whose brains
have been tinkered with under the spell
of drill, saw, and scalpel.

In some cases, this may include the brain's removal,
the lifting of a neural gist of consciousness
(minus its spark and snap) from the skull's receptacle,
leading to its weighty scrutiny on a stainless-steel scale
like an offering to the lab-coated gods.

Brainectomy: the carving out of a foreign object you object to,
lodged and growing within the bone confines of your head,
pressing against your perceptions,
making you giddy with stardust when it rains,
forcing you to see the night in brightest day,
folding you into a crumple of muscle & bone.

2.

She said they wanted to operate again.
This would be the fourth in as many months.

The first was to remove that foreign object: a tumor.

the second was to put in another foreign object: a stent
meant to drain the mounting fluid in the cavity
the removal of the tumor had made.

The third was to fix the stent, which didn't fix
the fluid building in the cavity made by the removal
of the tumor, which pressed against her perceptions
of the world, putting her into a weak and dizzy tizzy,
which once again she found herself in owing

to the continued pressure that the third fix
of the unworkable stent did not fix, so the need
for a fourth fix to re-fix that which wasn't fixed,
once again, entailed the unfixing of her life.
♫ *And the green grass grew all around, all around,*
and the green grass grew ♫—like a tumor.

3.

All this began long, long, ago,
twenty years before,
when the very first tumor appeared,
and then the second,
which arrived ten years after,
was also cut away from all that was
motor and memory.

Then along came the third and final tumor
like a Christmas turkey waiting to be carved.

4.

She said they wanted to operate again.
This would be the fourth in as many months.

She told me she wanted to say, *No! No more!*
— and would I agree to it? As if I could decide
how much suffering another should bear,
as if my leave was one of the gifts
she needed to leave this world
where belief in life had become blind to her life,
though everyone could see just fine.

The Mystery

It's not the Hindu gods swirling around
in my head like cartoon characters showing
the complexities of the human spirit.
Behind each belief lies a small, unseen,
wish waiting to be fulfilled, squirreling
away its nuts for the mother of all winters.
It's only when it gets out of hand,
and all the characters in my head
suddenly break out in song and dance
that I know it's finally the end,
and everyone is happy they are one
with the universe. I can see that
in the consonance of their movements,
the unison of their song, and I look
at the ground in time to see even the ants
line dancing to the same beat.
They, too, are happy about the end,
because the awful human shuffle and stomp
can't crush the true body of their belief
that soon they will return freed at last
from their carapace of karma
and the purgatory of past lives,
so they may, once again, continue
to climb the ladder of human frailty
toward perfection and the formless
no-step dance which is the universe.

The Legacy of Elms

What I remember from childhood
was not so much their stateliness—their
hallelujahs of upward limbs poising
in procession up the long avenues—

but the day they came down: how the tall
plumb ranks they formed suddenly tumbled
into jumbles of sticks and stumps, and the for-
granted shade they gave left forever,

so even the cloudiness of that day
had the blinding effect of making
the world too bright to really see.

Decades later, I found one last tree, alone,
in a field, its limbs lifting the air back up
as if loss had no weight, no substance at all.

The Sound of War

For Farideh Hassanzadeh

I try to grasp what it's like to live
where war is your neighbor,
the bomb next door.

You wait for its knock
to borrow your last cup of sugar.
Instead, it takes your house
and the child once within you.

I try to trace the etymology of that sound,
where the shrapnel of its consonants unwrap
from around the uncontainable
nucleus of its one deadly syllable.

In the end, there is no word for it,
no word small enough to fit
inside the human mouth.

My Father's Helmet

In the trunk in the attic of my real father's
imaginary house, I reach with both hands
and lift out his lead-scarred helmet,

I look deep into the olive-drab darkness,
where the air holds its vacant wisdom,
then place the helmet on my head,

and in that silent surge of armor,
the past I supposed becomes apparent
and I begin to think like my father.

I begin to smell the same rat-like fear
which curled like smoke in his nostrils
on the last day he wore it. I begin to feel

the staccato tap of death slamming his head
down, hear its leaden pings & splats
as it caroms off the helmet's metal shell.

I can even see the same daffodils he saw,
their sunlit heads bobbing & weaving
outside a machine gun's line of fire, waving

beside the slit-smile of the gray, hive-shaped nest,
where the gunner spits out his bullets like furious
bees searching to sting anything that moves.

I see, now, desperate for life, he had no choice
but to cradle the emptiness of it in his arms,
to crawl that perilous distance toward daffodils

and my mother's bed, praying he could shed
along the way fear's useless skin,
while, above, the bees searched the air.

Father's Day

You need to stop drying
the wife's dishes and put

the towel over your tired shoulder
like a matador's cape;

you need to say, *¡Olé!* when the sudden thought
of an invisible man comes to mind.

You need to step through the screen door
into the steamy, green & indigo yard,

past the rusting swing set, its bubbled paint
peeling off the brown silence of its bones,

and past the now rickety tree house,
still cradled in the dying limbs of the old oak,

and on through the hole in the hedge,
as though all along you expected this:

the fireflies coming to take you back.

Berceuses

We sat in the dimmed kitchen light
as everyone else began to go *au lit*
like players sauntering offstage.

Then, from under the table with its cracked,
yellowed vinyl, punctuated by nondescript
flowers, the man I considered *mon père*

would pull out his gallon jug of wine,
pouring yet another wistful, jelly jar full
to wet his whistle before he sang.

First, *La Marseillaise* would rasp out
à mi-voix from his throat, then all
the similar hymns of guts and glory,

each with their own *beaux gestes:*
standards I can still hear—fluttering
standards pointing in my mind's eye

toward some *champs élysees* where heroic
warriors squatted and sang, swaying their
goblets sideways in sync to every clink,

and the tremolo of their dying voices,
captured in one, final, patriotic pitch, always
ended in a hushed drumroll of dreams.

So Let Us Call Him Homer

Four AM and I awake, pulling him up
to this sudden surface like a crabber
on a shaky dock with bait and line.
HIPAA forbids me to say his name—
even if I could remember it—so let us
call him Homer, bard of silence and stuffed
emotions, blinded by the alcohol in his life.

I see him grasping at wet straws as he
gropes through the darkness of his days
seeking solace from having a father,
who took his belt strap to Homer's back
every time the old man got drunk,

which was every day of Homer's early life.
And so, his epic became an unmetered stew
of anger and anguish doused each day
with any sauce that would soften the hard
memories he couldn't pluck from the strings
of his lyre.
        Now, as I arise in the absence
of light impeding my own odyssey out of bed,
I fumble to my desk and scribble out this one poem
to commemorate what I'd almost forgot:

about the group I ran in detox, when Homer lost it,
and in the raw, breaking baritone of all he couldn't
sing, Homer cried out the scarred notes of his story
to the stunned ears of everyone there.

The Elephant in the Room

Thick skinned, wrinkled and gray,
it sits surrounded by eggshells
you must walk on but not disturb.

Deus of denial and false complacency,
ancient demon of faltering families,
just when you think it's disappeared
like an obsolete religion, fear of god,

out of the corner of your eye, you see
its long reach snake up to sniff you out,
you see it sit again in the easy chair
by the standing lamp, cross its legs,

all big-eared and selectively deaf,
then snap open the paper like a whip,
make you jump—crush the shells.

Pressure Cooker

For years after I could still see
the round stain of its statement

on the kitchen ceiling,
and in my mind's eye

the yellowed noodles
of chicken soup

are hanging there as well:
a salty broth still dripping.

But most of all I remember
ma mère's sharp cry

after the slow boil's expansion
and the inarticulate sound

of locked metal surrendering
as the cooker hissed then

un-clammed in full voice.
Only the lid escapes

my memory. Where did it go?
And that sudden unsealing

of a tightly fastened world . . .

Fugue

Shift change and I am here
working for the first time
the locked ward for adolescents.
The afternoon sun descends
like a dubious gift,
stretching the shadows
behind the short lives
of everyone in its light.
Kids mill about bawling
like street hawkers selling
the bounce and squeeze
of their stress. A magma
bubbles beneath, while staff,
almost as young, attempt to solidify
the only eruption the kids may make
down to the courtyard
for basketball and Frisbee.

For a moment, I am still here,
appearing as vigilant as my co-worker,
the skittering back and forth
of her eyes trying to count heads.

For a moment I am still there,
amid the slap and shuffle of slippers,
amid the shouts and silence of their banter,
the buried wounds of abuse and abandonment,
the buried hurt of failed placements
in foster home after foster home,
all of them clambering in a relentless
commotion against the past—until,
a soft-and-untouchable-front slides in
covering me like a deafening blanket,
and the din its silence hides
diminishes into a thin hum.

Voices   flutter away,   a gray,   still   blur   arrives,
even the light,   tilting   through the window,
winks out   like a   failed   bulb,   and   there is
<u>no</u>   <u>one</u>   <u>here</u>   existing in this   mute   moment,
this now-diaphanous   place,   a   limbo-veil,
where the sabbatical   from color,   feeling,
and sound,   commends this   shrouded self
to this   blank,   numb,   burial-at-sea,   this
limbic zero   of time,   memory   and place.

Fairy Tale for a Young Inpatient

Down, down, way down, at the very bottom
of the old wishing well, the one with the broken crank,

no rope, and no pail, the one still covered
by the quaint, scant roof meant to keep other things out,

down, down to where the memories you keep lie
at the bottom like tarnished pennies, one day,

there will appear a splendid fish, as red and gold
as your fabulous cape, my princess, my forlorn one.

You will see it swim in the deep, distorting murk
we all wish to forget, fluttering its fins like a fledgling,

testing its way out of the well, and you will drop a line, a strangling
thread from your cape, unspun in desperation,

trying, once more, to reach beyond the bottom
to where there are no memories. But, you will

catch this fish, instead, reeling it in like a new story
worth telling, unnoticed until now, though

it has always been there flickering about between the dull coins.
And after you pull up this fish with its sparkling gossamer fins

you will wrap it gently in the matching
colors of your cape, cradle it in your scarred arms

all the way up the narrow, insufficient pass
of your past with its many twists and turns,

along the whole cruelty of that journey,
then finally down the other side to a calm place,

where the lake water licks the shore in little waves.
There, you will kneel down and surrender

all that you've carried into that clear water,
stretching yourself out to swim with the fish,

the beautiful one you rescued.

An Incidental List of Loss

The squall at birth, though its echo
continues throughout your whole life
becoming birdsong, the bear huffing
at the backside of the blackberry patch,
the shuffle of deer in autumn woods,
wishing themselves to the deep thicket
they may never reach, the sudden gasp
of lovers in the dark, the mother you finally
met at the last minute, the watch she gave you,
stopped at a moment you weren't looking,
the present even now in the past, the hiccup
of time lurching out of the place you will forget,
dark hands jerking across a clock's white face—
the watch!—the watch!—in which drawer did you . . . ?

A Game of Cards

Night finally came. I had already
turned on the overhead light
illuminating the room,
its different shades of gray,
when my patient suggested
that we play a game of cards.

I thought about this.
I had long ago given up on chance
and was steering my life
toward the certainties I had begun
to learn were truly there.

These were not certainties as one knows facts, today,
with their tangible logic as hard as rock
and as immutable as the progression of multiplication tables
always moving toward their unavoidable answers.
Those were the mental traps of a mundane mind.

Instead, my certainties were a kind of wisdom,
which emitted from a veiled, capuchin-clad figure
that I noticed followed behind me
wherever I went.

At each moment of indecision on my part,
when I would find myself at a crossroads
where the vanishing point to each choice
showed nothing but a vague promise
diminishing into the distance,

it would whisper to me, imparting
its knowledge into one ear or the other
(it had no true preference)
always telling me the whys-and-therefores
of the options I was contemplating.

Of course, no one else saw this.
Why should they? The figure
was obviously there only for me.

But to try and explain to you what it was
I should start by saying what it was not.
Although it was wont to speak anything
more than the advice it gave,
it was not a guardian angel.
This much it had confessed to me.

Nonetheless, I began to look upon it
as a higher force from a not so ancient past,
whose physical and spiritual being had been
so deformed by the misfortunes of its own life,

that in its current configuration it had willed itself
to maintain a presence in the nether wake
all mortals make moving through the world
and to advise the mortal it followed
how to thwart the tragedies and mishaps
the figure had already lived.

The overhead light flickered once,
and my patient interrupted my thoughts
insisting we begin our game.

My poor, delusional patient,
whose white garb and guileless expression
belied the true wiles of his mind.

He laid his first card down, telling me
in his earnest, matter of fact manner
how he would beat me, that his sense of numbers
and his memory were better than mine,
so, for him, this, too, was no game of chance.

A Brief Explanation of the Psychotic Universe

This is how it works: the invisible
cause and effect of the universe,
that Big Bang no one has ever heard,
emits its waves of singular commands.

Then the voices ripple through the cosmos,
one by one, whispering their secret orders,
which only I can hear, for I am Cassandra.
I see them slipping into my ear, shifting
with each surreptitious twist of air, skating
the thin line between wind and waft until,
with a flutter, a momentary lull settles
into my head telling me it's time.

Friends, penitents, suffering pilgrims,
all blessed in your hospital blues,
listen, for I have heard the universe,
the first echoes of its birth, nearing
louder and louder with each new gust,
and I alone have escaped to tell you.

Note to the Mental Hospital Timekeeper

Dear Bob,

Today, I subbed at the hospital school,
babysitting class after class,
teaching the kids nothing—the ones
who live across the street
in the group homes the hospital runs.

As you can see from the time clock,
ADP provides both you and me,
it took the allotted six point five hours
before the kids and I gathered up
our coats and hats, calling it a day,
and they trudged back to the locked doors
of their houses, and I climbed the stairs
to the locked door of my garret,
where I write you this poem
instead of my usual email—not about
the extra money I am due—but about
the grains of sand, which seemed
to sift through my fingers, today,
each grain chafing at another life
each child imagines living,
and about the heaviness
weighing on them, drooping
their shoulders like sand bags
the residents of some river town carry
to make the embankments they need
to hold back the imminent flood.

Nonetheless,
please remember to credit me
the higher pay rate I am in fact due,
if only for offering my empty hand,
then for filling it with pencils
I personally sharpened, cursing
the pencil maker for their off-center leads,
as I then gave each student their own wand
to calculate the magic of wisdom
and to mark down the answers
they are trying to find: the true values
of the algebraic x's in the countless
disappointments that make up
the lopsided equations of their lives.

Tomorrow, I'll sub again,
and I promise to send you
another reminder. Until then,
keep the home fires burning
and the old time-clock well oiled.
We'll never know—will we?—
when the electric world will fail
and the spark of connection dies.

The March Hare

It was almost the end of the shift,
someone on the muzak above was playing
a bebop version of *Matchmaker*,
when one of the patients sauntered over.
Slouching in front of me, he hooked his thumbs
into his belt loops, spread his legs apart
and rocked back and forth copping
a kind of wise guy, cowboy attitude.
He said he wanted to leave, and he understood
the best way to get *outta Dodge* was to get
married, and then, he could leave tonight.
I could call him a cab, but first,
I had to find him a woman to marry.

He must have been sizing me up all night.
I'd been hanging out in a nice comfy
armchair, with a modern, cartoonish
pattern of outsized flowers in a soothing,
non-violent color scheme that went well
with the rest of the unit's subtle decor.
The tune, piping down from the ceiling,
changed to something I couldn't recognize,
but I was still feeling pretty good: no woman
in my life, music in my ears, and until then,
a quiet night in the tilting house of the hare.

By now, he was looming over me,
intently waiting for my answer. All
six foot six of him, and by his girth,
a good four hundred and fifty pounds—
maybe more. . . . *Well,* I said, as I stood up
to my full five foot nine and a half inches,
*let me look into this. I've got to enquire
to see who's available. It might take a . . .*

moment or two, but I'll get right back,
and I sauntered out of reach whistling
whatever tune was playing—maybe
Hit the Road, Jack with a fast alto sax
squealing out like a tire or *Fifty Ways*
to Leave Your Lover, something memorable
for one man's desire but not another's.

When I Come to Visit, You Appear

from the invisible part of your kitchen
as I stand inside slipping off my shoes
in the alcove. You're dressed casually

which belies the length of time you've spent
choosing with exactitude: slacks, blouse
and sometimes a scarf-like choker

to complement your top. You smile as
you approach sweeping your glasses off
so they won't hit mine when we kiss

and fit our bodies against each other
as if we were the last pieces
to a puzzle we've just put together.

Reflection

You rescue it from behind a veil of clothes:
a mirror framed in dark veneer with a band
of gold around the edge. The glass, now turned
milky and spotted from tarnished silver
flaking off its back, stares out, a blind eye.

The wall behind the bathroom sink, where you
wanted to hang it, got sold along with the house
(you can't remember how many houses ago),
and you've moved yet again to where neither you
nor the mirror seem to fit. Why does anyone—

except to behold yourself through that special
frame, which caught your fancy, its beveled glass
seeming as if you were gazing into a jewel,
seeing at last the preciousness of yourself.

Butterfly

For Betsy

Since I have no long-handled net
to capture what I want to offer you,
I turn to Dunn's poem *Instead of You.*
In it, he's invented a butterfly to distract
from the reader he doesn't name, whom
he's hidden on the page as a faint watermark
beneath the butterfly's paper-thin wings.
I watch the wings flutter their dust
toward the foolscap corners of his poem,

and I decide to take his butterfly, pluck it
right off his page and put it on mine,
make it the symbol I will use for us.
I even tell you it's my own invention
as I spread and pin it in all its colorful
splendor on this page you're reading
right this moment, and you're not
a graying shadow smudged beneath
this butterfly like an afterthought.

Now I am ready. I feel as if the gist
of what I could thrust with my pen
would replenish that hollow, thoracic hole
we've both known, you and I, that place
collectors of such metaphors have been
trying to fill with this last specimen—
too fragile to ever put our finger on—but
which would complete them (and us), so then,
the glass lid could close over their lives.

The Eagle Outside

Hunched on a bare-bones limb
outside the staff room window,
its dark shoulders paler in the mist,
we could barely see its white head,
against the gray vagueness of the air.
Morning hadn't burned away
all that hovered over the river,
and we were talking patients until
the night charge changed the subject,
pointing to the bird through the pane
behind us. We shifted back to his
report, and when we turned at the end,
it was gone, delving deep into that
blind part of day for a bright fish.

Notes

"Meditation on Your Final Moment": *soulagement* is French for relief, and *salut* has two meanings in French, the first is as a greeting and the second meaning is salvation.

"A Different Color of Sun": *bons mots* means witticisms in French. I ran into a car on my racing bike at full speed, which, needless to say, was physically disastrous. The limited mobility of my left arm is probably more due to my neck injuries and the nerve which leads to that arm from my neck rather than any injuries my brain suffered . . . poetic license.

"Self-Portrait with *Trache*": In the hospital I learned *trache* is a medical slang/shorthand term for tracheostomy tube. I unfortunately learned the hard way.

"*Berceuses*": means lullabies in French; "*au lit*" means to bed, "*mon père*" my father; "*La Marseillaise*" is the French national anthem; "*champs élysées*" the mythic Elysian fields where warriors went after death, "*beaux gestes*" noble or gallant acts, and lastly, *à mi-voix* is the equivalent of *sotto voce*, in a quiet voice.

"So Let Us Call Him Homer": HIPAA (The Health Insurance Portability and Accountability Act of 1996) among other things, forbids people working in healthcare from disclosing information about or identifying a patient in care without written permission of the patient. This doesn't mean one can't mention the particulars of a case as long as it is mentioned in a manner where it can't be identified to that person.

"Pressure Cooker": *ma mère* means my mother.

"Fairy Tale for a Young Inpatient": I have worked for 15+ years in a mental hospital as part of the nursing staff caring for the safety and well-being of inpatients. The two things that staff have to watch out for on an adolescent inpatient unit are attempts by

the kids to impulsively hang or strangle themselves by unraveling
their clothes and to make sure that a patient doesn't find any
sharp objects to self-harm with usually by cutting their arms.
The physical pain caused by the self-harming distracts from and/
or relieves the emotional and psychological pain that a patient is
experiencing.

"A Brief Explanation of the Psychotic Universe": "Hospital
blues" are the blue paper scrubs all patients are asked to wear
during admission, while their personal effects and clothing
are "contrabanded" (searched) to determine if they have any
physically dangerous objects and/or drugs among their effects
which patients are not allowed to bring to the locked unit, where
they will be treated. There's a long list of what is considered
harmful contraband including belts, strings in clothing and any
sharp objects.

"Note to the Mental Hospital Timekeeper": Automatic Data
Processing, Inc., commonly known by its New York Stock
Exchange symbol, *ADP*, is a provider of human resources
management software and services. There is an online login
portal where workers and their timekeepers at the hospital can
verify the time clock swipes. In that portal on the electronic
time sheet there is also a place where the timekeeper can make
notations about pay rates according to the job you are performing
and adjust the time swiped in if one happened to make a mistake
swiping in (or forgot). Although most people didn't, I used to
work different jobs at different pay rates. As a substitute teacher
in the hospital school, I was paid much more than when I worked
as a mental health worker under nursing supervision on an
inpatient unit. Thus, when I clocked in, I often needed to email
the timekeeper to tell him which job I was working so he could
credit me the pay rate which applied to that particular job.

"The March Hare": "To be as 'mad as a March hare' is an English
idiomatic phrase derived from the observed antics, said to
occur only in the March breeding season, of the European Hare

Lepus europaeus. The phrase is an allusion that can be used to refer to any other animal or human who behaves in the excitable and unpredictable manner of a 'March hare.' A long-held view is that the hare will behave strangely and excitedly throughout its breeding season, which in Europe peaks in the month of March. This odd behavior includes boxing at other hares, jumping vertically for seemingly no reason and generally displaying abnormal behavior." (Wikipedia) This used to be the Wikipedia explanation for the term "March hare." I love it so much I quoted it in its entirety before someone changed the explanation.

Acknowledgments

I've dedicated this book in part to Patricia Fargnoli, who, before she died, extended her love and friendship to me and helped with many of the poems in this collection. In addition, I would like to thank Maggie Smith for her guidance in an early version of this collection, showing me the importance of some of the poems, and Molly Peacock, who also advised me through a later version. Also, I would like to thank Rachel Hadas and her workshop for advice on some poems in this collection. But most of all, I want to bring to my readers' attention, Betsy Whittaker, my muse, and thank her for her love, support, advice and to whom this collection as well as some of its poems are dedicated. I would also like to thank Ben and Tamarah Rockwood and their team at Bainbridge Island Press for believing in my work and for their compassionate patience in transmogrifying this collection into a beautiful book. Finally, I would like to thank the following literary journals for publishing these poems:

The American Journal of Poetry: "*Brainectomy*," & "The Moral of the Story"

American Poetry Journal: "The Steel Gray Nail"

Avatar Review: "The Black Wolf of Your Past," "Hallway," & "The Sound of War,"

Crosswinds Poetry Journal: Earlier versions of "The Ladder," "The Eagle Outside" and "Variations on Mozart's Rondo in A Minor"

COG Magazine: "Pressure Cooker"

The Hamilton Stone Review: An earlier version of "Another Man's Treasure"

International Poetry Review: An earlier version of "My Father's Helmet"

Meniscus: "A Pure Bodiless Sound"

Naugatuck River Review: "Note to the Mental Hospital Timekeeper" & "Crumple Zone"

Nine Muses: "A Brief Explanation of the Psychotic Universe" & "*Berceuses*"

The Nonconformist: An earlier version of "Self-Portrait with *Trache*" entitled "Untitled"

ONE: "The Elephant in the Room"

One Art: "A Father's Lament" & "A Candle For"

Prachya Review: "Fairy Tale for a Young Inpatient," & "A Game of Cards"

Rat's Ass Review: "Amelia's Cat," "The Legacy of Elms," & "An Incidental List of Loss," "Vicissitudes," "The Sunshine," and "At the Chemo Clinic"

Sheila-Na-Gig: "June Burial," "Butterfly," "Big Nose Blond," and "The Anthropology of Old Age"

San Pedro River Review: "Fugue," & "Pine Heights Rehab"

SOLSTICE: "A Different Color of Sun"

Turtle Island: "Snow," An earlier version of "Landscape with Still Life," entitled "Revocable Beauty"

Valparaiso Poetry Review: "The Gospel of Numbers Not in Service" & an earlier version of "Meditation on Your Final Moment" entitled "The Unadulterated Moment"

Verse-Virtual: for reprinting final versions of the following poems: "Fairy Tale for a Young Inpatient," "The Ladder," "The Black Wolf of Your Past," "The March Hare," "Meditation on Your Final Moment," "The Moral of the Story," and "Note to the Mental Hospital Timekeeper."

The Worcester Review: "The People Inside Me:"

"The Ladder" appeared on the Mass Poetry website: *The Hard Work of Hope*

A number of poems in this collection have also appeared in my previously published chapbook, *Notes to the Mental Hospital Timekeeper*. They are: "Fairy Tale for a Young Inpatient," "The Ladder," "A Brief Explanation of the Psychotic Universe," "A Game of Cards," "The Black Wolf of Your Past," "The Elephant in the Room," "The March Hare," "Pressure Cooker," "Fugue," "The Moral of the Story," and "Note to the Mental Hospital Timekeeper."

About the Author

Tim Mayo is the author of two previous full-length poetry collections, *The Kingdom of Possibilities* (2009), and *Thesaurus of Separation* (2016) and two chapbooks, *The Loneliness of Dogs* (2008) and *Notes to the Mental Hospital Timekeeper* (2019). He holds an ALB, *cum laude*, from Harvard University and an MFA from Bennington College. A ten-time Pushcart Prize Nominee, and a two-time finalist for the Paumanok Award, Mayo is also the recipient of three Vermont Writers Fellowships from the Vermont Studio Center, as well as being a finalist for the Eric Hoffer Book Award and the Montaigne Medal. He lives in Brattleboro, VT, where he worked for fifteen years at the Brattleboro Retreat, a mental institution, as both a teacher and a mental health worker, and where he is also a founding member and organizer of the Brattleboro Literary Festival.